I SPY
CHRISTMAS

A BOOK OF
PICTURE
RIDDLES

Photographs by Walter Wick

Riddles by Jean Marzollo

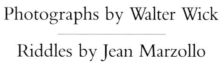

Hippo

For my parents, Betty and Peter Wick

———————

W.W

Also available in book shops

I SPY: A BOOK OF PICTURE RIDDLES
I SPY MYSTERY: A BOOK OF PICTURE RIDDLES
I SPY SCHOOL DAYS: A BOOK OF PICTURE RIDDLES

Book design by Carol Devine Carson

Scholastic Children's Books,
Commonwealth House, 1-19 New Oxford Street,
London WC1A 1NU, UK
A division of Scholastic Ltd
London ~ New York ~ Toronto ~ Sydney ~ Auckland

First published by Scholastic Inc, 1992
This paperback edition first published in the UK by Scholastic Ltd, 1997

Text copyright © Jean Marzollo, 1992
Photographs copyright © Walter Wick, 1992

Hardback ISBN: 0 590 54099 8
Paperback ISBN: 0 590 11232 5

Typeset by Rapid Reprographics
Printed in Hong Kong

2 4 6 8 10 9 7 5 3 1

TABLE OF CONTENTS

Picture riddles fill this book;
Turn the pages! Take a look!

Use your mind, use your eye;
Read the rhymes and play I SPY!

I spy an angel, a silver clock,
Santa on a sleigh, a proud peacock;

A frog on a leaf, a chubby teddy bear,
Black and white keys, and a yellow-red pear.

I spy a horse and three glitter shells,
A fine-pointed star, and two silver bells;

One golden ring, a little white cat,
A swan and a bear and a thimble hat.

I spy a snowman, three hens in a row,
A drumstick, a rabbit, a small yellow bow;

An almond, a magnet, a sea gull, a chick,
A hammer, a bus, and a wooden toothpick.

I spy a jingle bell, two birds of blue,
A bunny, a star, and Santa's red shoe;

An old-fashioned key, two small striped stones,
A red shoelace, and seven pine cones.

I spy a wagon, J on a block,
A smart ladybird and a heart-shaped lock;

Two snowy mittens, three pairs of gloves,
A monkey named Socks, and two turtledoves.

I spy a house, a drum, and a clock,
Three fat pigs, and a squirrel-tail sock;

A string of lights, a belt with a B,
A criss-cross heart, and a broken tree.

I spy a thimble, a white Christmas kitten,
Two fuzzy chickens, a little green mitten;

Three paper clips, an ornament house,
A bottle of glue, and a nutty brown mouse.

I spy a goose, a cat lying down,
A paintbrush, an acorn, a chick, and a clown;

A little white church, a bird on a block,
Six musical bears, and a key for a lock.

I spy three dominoes, a corn on the cob,
A zebra, a duck, a little green frog;

A pink clothespeg, a steeple on a church,
A little blue plane, and a bird on a perch.

I spy a fish, a brown hatband,
A horse, a cow, and a pointing hand;

A five-bar gate, a bell-ringing bear,
A tiny birdhouse, and Santa in a chair.

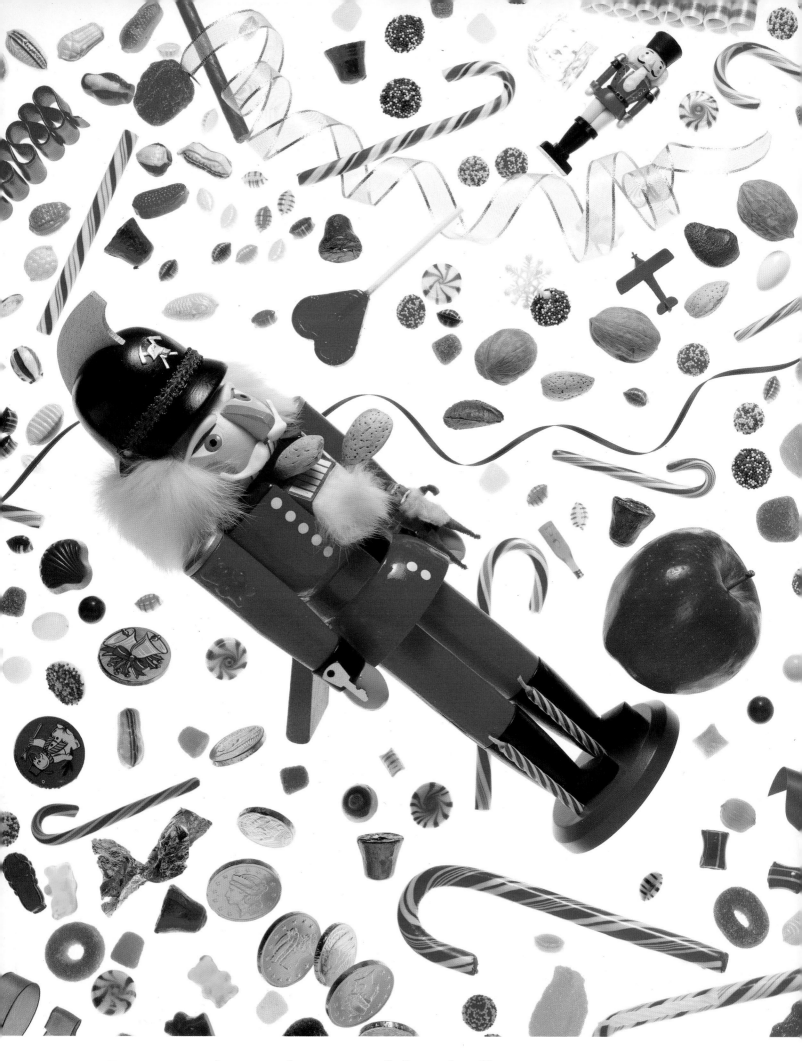

I spy an ice cube, a golden bell,
A carrot for a nose, a chocolate shell;

A hatchet at work, a bottle, a key,
A pine cone, a plane, and a Christmas tree.

I spy a cockerel, a Santa with a cane,
The shadow of a star, a popcorn chain;

Two fancy coaches, a ribbon of blue,
Some musical notes, and JOY 2 U, too.

I spy a glove, a horse, and a gate,
A silver coin, the shadow of a skate;

A shovel, a lamb, a Christmas tree light,
Five jacks, and a dove in the dark silent night.

EXTRA CREDIT RIDDLES

"Find Me" Riddle

Find me with the bears; I sit on their shelf;
I'm in every picture; I'm Santa's _____.

Find the Pictures that Go with These Riddles:

I spy a gumdrop, a laughing clown,
Shoes for a baby, and a golden crown.

I spy MOTHER, a bear with a broom,
A doll and a phone and a small mushroom.

I spy a chicken, a mouse, and a horn,
An R and a Z, and an ear of corn.

I spy a teacup, and orange tangerine,
Seven chewy bears, and a green jellybean.

I spy a rabbit, a spider in the sky,
Seven reindeer, and an angel on high.

I spy a mouse, two kites, and a spoon,

A yellow gumdrop, and an angel with a moon.

I spy a trumpet, an empty nut shell,

Four letter blocks, and the word Noel.

I spy an acorn, a button, a bow,

A fancy gold egg, and a basket in the snow.

I spy a snowman, a colourful clown,

A wintry scene, and a king with a crown.

I spy a pine cone, a tin Christmas tree,

A little gold wrench, and a capital G.

I spy a necktie, some sweets in a chair,

Two horses that rock, and a hatbox bear.

I spy a streetlight, a soldier in blue,

Four candles, a pan, and a little red shoe.

I spy a queen and a ballet slipper,

Three bells, a truck, and a Little Dipper.

Write Your Own Picture Riddles

There are many more hidden objects and many more possibilities for riddles in this book. Write some rhyming picture riddles yourself, and try them out with friends.

Special Acknowledgements

First of all, we'd like to thank Grace Maccarone, senior editor, and Bernette Ford, editorial director of Cartwheel Books, for their generous enthusiasm and guidance in producing *I Spy: A Book of Picture Riddles* and *I Spy Christmas: A Book of Picture Riddles*. We'd also like to thank Jean Feiwel, Barbara Marcus, Edie Weinberg, John Illingworth, Lenora Todaro, and all the other people at Scholastic who have supported our *I Spy* books.

We'd like to thank our agent, Molly Friedrich of The Aaron M. Priest Literary Agency, for her wit, wisdom, and willingness to solve problems creatively and thoroughly.

We'd like to thank artists Missy Stevens and Tommy Simpson for letting us use their extraordinary collections of antique teddy bears, antique ornaments, and hand-crafted Christmas decorations.

And finally, we'd like to thank Dora Jonassen for the cookies, Evan G. Hughes for evergreens, Christopher M. Hayes and Linda Bayette for help with *Santa's Workshop*, Verde Antiques for various props in *Window Shopping*, Katherine O'Donnell and Marianne Alibozak for their photo assistance, and Linda Cheverton-Wick for her superb artistic eye.

Walter Wick and Jean Marzollo